Thank you for purchasing *If I Could Grow a Tree*. The idea ca[...] dinner table with my wife Jody and our three boys, Kyle, Ryan and Breyden. We began by just asking the simple question: "if I could grow a tree?". On many nights, we had lots of fun imagining different thoughts for trees. The ideas kept growing and I decided to make a list in the hope of someday writing a book that would be educational and fun. Along the way, I was fortunate to find Susie Johnson to illustrate the book. Her talents not only brought the ideas to life, she was able to add great touches, such as the Earth Day t-shirt on the little boy sitting under an ice cream tree. I hope that while reading the book, you will find trees such as the numbers or shapes trees educational. Other trees, such as the camping and zoo trees are meant to build childrens' creative sides by letting their imaginations run free. I enjoyed the time with our boys, asking them to name the shapes, count and recognize the numbers, or find animals on the zoo tree. I hope you will like it just the same.

Jeff Peitzmeier

IF I COULD GROW A TREE
by Jeff Peitzmeier

# If I could *grow* a TREE

# What would it BE?

by

**Jeff Peitzmeier**

Illustrations by Susie Johnson

# If I could *grow* a **TREE. . .**

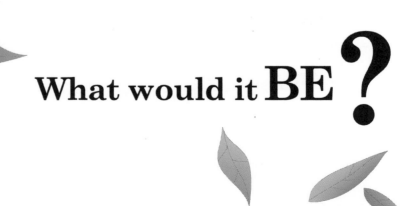

## What would it **BE**?

# *an* ALPHABET TREE. . .

so I could learn my ABC's

# If I could *grow* a TREE. . .

## What would it BE?

# *a* SHAPES TREE. . .

SQUARE

HEXAGON

RECTANGLE

CIRCLE

DIAMOND

OVAL

TRIANGLE

Because CIRCLES, SQUARES & TRIANGLES
are what I would see !

# If I could *grow* a TREE. . .

What would it BE?

# a NUMBERS TREE...

so we can count the stars: one, two, three.

# If I could *grow* a TREE. . .

## What would it BE?

# a COLORS TREE. . .

because it's fun to ride a rainbow & shout with glee!

red   orange   yellow   green   blue   violet

Rainbow PAINT

If I could *grow* a **TREE**. . .

What would it **BE**?

a ZOO TREE. . .

with all of the
animals for you
and me to see!

If I could *grow* a **TREE...**

**What would it BE?**

a PET TREE. . .

with friendly animals to PLAY with me.

# If I could *grow* a **TREE. . .**

**What would it BE?**

a CAMPING TREE. . .

with room for THREE!

# If I could *grow* a TREE. . .

## What would it BE?

# *a* VEGETABLE TREE. . .

because I love to eat my
carrots, broccoli and peas.

If I could *grow* a TREE. . .

What would it BE ?

# a FRUIT TREE...

because apples, bananas & strawberries are soooo yummy!

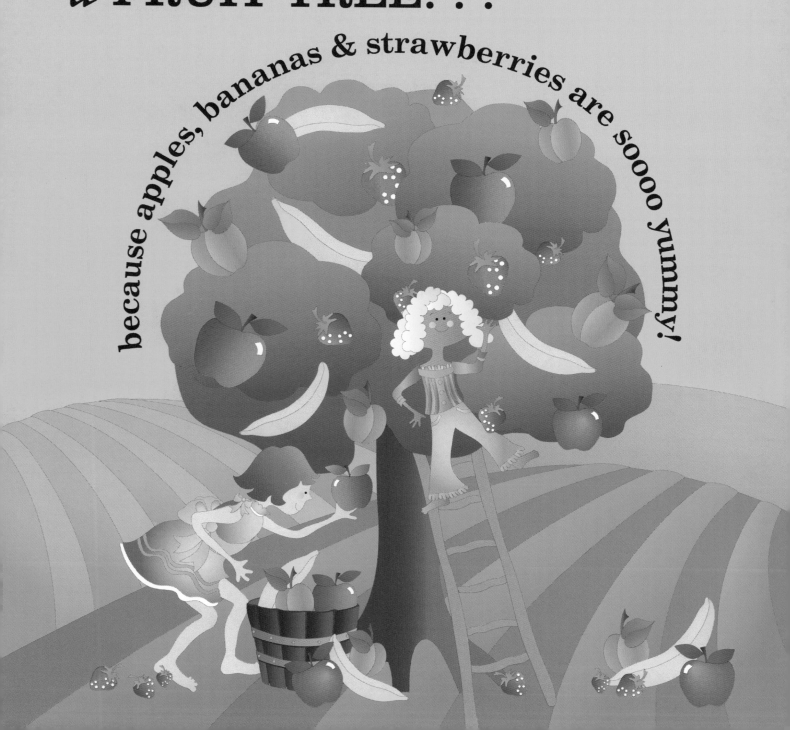

# If I could *grow* a TREE. . .

## What would it BE?

# If I could *grow* a TREE. . .

## What would it BE?

# THE END
## ?

29110321R00017

Made in the USA
Charleston, SC
02 May 2014